János Pilinszky

THE DESERT OF LOVE
Selected Poems
Translated by
János Csokits and Ted Hughes
Introduced by Ted Hughes
with a memoir by
Ágnes Nemes Nagy

Anvil Press Poetry

Selected Poems published by Carcanet Press in 1976
Revised and enlarged edition published in 1989
by Anvil Press Poetry Ltd
69 King George Street London SE10 8PX

This edition copyright © Péter Kovács 1989
Translations © János Csokits and Ted Hughes 1976, 1989
Introduction © Ted Hughes 1976, 1989
'A Very Different Poet' copyright © Ágnes Nemes Nagy 1981

This book is published with
financial assistance from
The Arts Council of Great Britain

Set in Raleigh
by Calvert's Press
Printed in England
by the Arc & Throstle Press
Todmorden, Lancs

British Library Cataloguing in Publication Data
Pilinszky, János
 The desert of love : selected poems.
 I. Title II. Csokits, János III. Hughes, Ted
 894'.51113   PH3321.P5

 ISBN 0-85646-177-6
 ISBN 0-85646-178-4 Pbk

Some of these translations originally appeared in *Critical Quarterly, Lines Review* and *Modern Poetry in Translation*. The introductory essay appeared in *Poetry Nation* VI.

We thank the editors of *The New Hungarian Quarterly* for permission to reprint the essay by Ágnes Nemes Nagy, which first appeared in *NHQ* number 84 (1981).

The order of the poems is that of *Kráter* (Szépirodalmi Könyvkiadó, Budapest, 1976) and *Összegyűjtött Versei* edited by István Jelenits (Szépirodalmi Könyvkiadó, Budapest, 1987).

CONTENTS

INTRODUCTION by Ted Hughes / 7

from *Trapeze and Parallel Bars* (1940–1946)

Fish in the Net / 17
Trapeze and Parallel Bars / 18
Under the Winter Sky / 19
You Have Had to Suffer Rain and Cold / 20
What Underground Struggle / 21

from *On the Third Day* (1946–1958)

Sin / 23
World Grown Cold / 25
Complaint / 26
By the Time You Come / 27
Harbach 1944 / 28
The French Prisoner / 30
On the Wall of a KZ–Lager / 32
Passion of Ravensbrück / 33
Frankfurt / 34
Impromptu / 36
The Desert of Love / 37
Revelations VIII.7 / 38
Apocrypha / 39
Quatrain / 42
Under a Portrait / 43
Cold Wind / 44
Unfinished Past / 45
November Elysium / 46

from *Big City Icons* (1959–1970)

Epilogue / 47
Introitus / 49
Fable [detail from *KZ–Oratorio: Dark Heaven*] / 50

Big City Icons / 51
Van Gogh / 52
The Passion / 53
Just Like the Earth / 54

from *Splinters* (1971–1972)

As I Was / 55
Crime and Punishment / 56
Exhortation / 57
The Prayer of Van Gogh / 58
My Coat of Arms / 59
Gradually / 60
Enough / 61
Straight Labyrinth / 62

from *Denouement* (1973–1974)

Meditation / 63
Stavrogin Takes His Leave / 64
Jewel / 65
Stavrogin Returns / 66

from *Crater* (1974–1975)

Pathography and Swansong / 67
Two / 68
Aquarium / 69
Crater / 70
Hommage à Sheryl Sutton I / 71

JÁNOS PILINSZKY: A VERY DIFFERENT POET
by Ágnes Nemes Nagy / 73

INTRODUCTION

Hungarians consider János Pilinszky to be one of their best poets. Sándor Weöres, a towering poet, and nobody's lipserver, called him 'our greatest'. He died in 1981.

His special quality is not easy to define. He recognisably belongs to that generation of East European poets which includes Herbert, Holub and Popa, but his differences draw any discussion of him into quite another context. Hungarians tend to set him a little outside their ordinary writers, and his poetry a little outside ordinary poetry. The reason for this is something essential to Pilinszky's character. Critical judgement cannot rest in the aesthetic excellence of his work: it inevitably ends up arguing the ethical-religious position of Pilinszky himself, not at all a simple one in modern Hungary or anywhere else, but one which his poems and other writings and his life define with such poignancy and authority that it confronts the critic with a problem—a private, existential challenge. His 'greatness', then, unlike Weöres', is not a greatness of imaginative and linguistic abundance. It has more to do with some form of spiritual distinction. The weight and unusual temper of his imagination and language derive from this.

The total volume of his poetry is quite slight. Up to 1970 the forms he used were traditional, varying only between tightness and looseness. Thereafter, his forms became externally free, and he became much more productive, though the poems themselves became more brief. The quality of his actual style is an essence, from the heart of his vision. It is direct, simple, even 'impoverished', but all Hungarians agree that it is a marvel of luminosity, unerring balance, sinuous music and intensity—a metal resembling nothing else. Through translation we can only try to imagine that (though working as closely with the originals as I have worked, one soon picks up a very distinct idea of it). But even a rough translation cannot completely blanket Pilinszky's unique vision of final things, or the urgency and depth and complexity of his poetic temperament.

He was born in Budapest in 1921. Certain known factors, which have had a vital influence on the mature form of his work, are worth mentioning. Perhaps one of the most decisive has been what might seem the most trivial. His syntax, for all its classical finish, is quite idiosyncratic. This can be felt clearly in a word-for-word crib—though it is less easy to translate further. Something elliptical in the connections, freakishly home-made, abrupt. It would not be going too far to say there is a primitive element in the way it grasps its subject. Yet this peculiarity is deeply part of its most sophisticated effects, and its truth. His own words give the best idea of it: 'Should someone ask, what after all is my poetic language, in truth I should have to answer: it is some sort of lack of language, a sort of linguistic poverty. I have learned our mother-tongue from my mother's elder sister, who met with an accident, was ill, and got barely beyond the stage of childlike stammering. This is not much. No doubt the world has added this and that, completely at random, accidentally, from very different workshops. This I *received*. And because the nice thing about our mother-tongue is exactly this fact, that we receive it, we do not want to add anything to it. We would feel it detrimental to do so. It would be as if we tried to improve our origin. But in art even such a poor language—and I must say this with the pride of the poor—can be redeemed. In art the deaf can hear, the blind can see, the cripple can walk, each deficiency may become a creative force of high quality' [from an interview— 1969]. This 'mother-tongue' and especially his attitude towards it, as he describes it here, is a revealing clue to Pilinszky's whole poetic character.

Another pervading factor, which almost every word he writes forces us to take into account, has been his Catholic upbringing and education. His continuing allegiance to certain aspects of Catholicism is evident in small things—his publishing many of his poems in Catholic journals, his joining the staff of the Catholic weekly *Új Ember* in 1957. The poems demonstrate, however, that his inner relationship to Catholicism is neither simple nor happy. He has been called a Christian poet, even a Catholic poet, and the increasing density of Catholic terminology and imagery in his work provides argument for this. But he rejected those labels absolutely. There is no doubt that he was above all a religious poet. A rather dreadful sun of religious awareness, a midnight sun, hangs over all his responses. But his loyalty to a different order of revelation—which at first seems a directly opposite and contradictory order—came first.

In 1944 he was conscripted for military service—just in time to be scooped up by the retreating German army. His last year of the war was spent moving from prison camp to prison camp in Austria and Germany.

Whatever he met in those camps evidently opened the seventh seal for Pilinszky. It was a revelation of the new man: humanity stripped of everything but the biological persistence of cells. After this experience there emerges, at the heart of his poems, a strange creature, 'a gasping, limbless trunk', savaged by primal hungers, among the odds and ends of a destroyed culture, waiting to be shot, or beaten to death, or just thrown on a refuse heap—or simply waiting in empty eternity. The shock of this initiation seems to have objectified and confirmed something he had known from childhood: the world of the camps became the world of his deepest, most private, poetic knowledge.

His first collection of poems appeared in 1946. It was a literary event in Hungary. He became leader, with Ágnes Nemes Nagy, of a new school of poets, and co-edited their magazine. Silence soon descended, however, and ten years had to pass before his poems began to emerge again. His second book, containing eighteen poems reprinted from his first, and thirty-four new poems, came out in 1959. It was acclaimed, at once, as the major achievement of a major writer.

Those comparatively few poems have gradually established his international reputation. It was recognised, from the start, that he spoke from the disaster-centre of the modern world. What was also clear, though, was that his words escaped, only with great effort, from an intensifying, fixed core of silence. The bleak, lonely, condemned one, at the heart of his poems, spoke less and less.

The next thirteen years added only sixteen new poems. Then in 1971 and 1974 two new collections, projecting a new line of development from what had seemed impossible to alter, contained ninety-seven fresh pieces. Yet these pieces, if anything, only deepened the fixity and silence. All are short, fragmentary. Some are hardly more than a sentence or couplet.

The first of these collections was titled *Splinters*—splinters, that is, from the cross. The title of the second can be translated *Denouement*. The change, however, was there. The mood and imagery of his earlier work survived through an inner tranformation which seemed uncompleted until, in 1975, he published *Space and Relationship*, a collection of poems interspersed with photographs of the sculptures of Erzsébet Schaár.

'I would like to write,' Pilinszky said, 'as if I had remained silent.' He is not alone among modern poets, particularly those of his generation and experience, in his obsession with personal silence. As it is used by those Indian saints who refuse to speak at all until the ultimate truth speaks through them, or as Socrates used it before his judges, or as Christ used it before his accusers, silence can be a resonant form of speech. Pilinszky, who is rarely ironic and never Messianic, makes us aware of another silence.

It is impossible not to feel that the spirit of his poetry aspires to the most naked and helpless of all confrontations: a Christ-like posture of crucifixion. His silence is the silence of that moment on the cross, after the cry.

The silence of artistic integrity 'after Auschwitz' is a real thing. The mass of the human evidence of the camps, and of similar situations since, has raised the price of 'truth' and 'reality' and 'understanding' beyond what common words seem able to pay. The European poets who have been formed by this circumstance are well known. They have only continued to write, when at all, with a seasoned despair, a minimal, much-examined hope, a special irony. But because he was as he was, consumed with religious awareness, Pilinszky shifted the problem into other dimensions—which are more traditional but also, perhaps, broader and older, more intimately relevant, more piercing.

This is not to suggest that his poetry is in its inmost spirit necessarily Christian. The poems are nothing if not part of an appeal to God, but it is a God who seems not to exist. Or who exists, if at all, only as he exists for the stones. Not Godlessness, but the immanence of a God altogether different from what dogmatic Christianity has ever imagined. A God of absences and negative attributes, quite comfortless. A God in whose creation the camps and modern physics are equally at home. But this God has the one Almightiness that matters: He is the Truth.

We come to this Truth only on the simplest terms: through what has been suffered, what is being suffered, and the objects that participate in the suffering. The mysterious thing is that in Pilinszky the naked, carnal, helpless quality of this truth is fused with the utmost spiritual intensity. The desolate furnishings of his vision are revealed by their radiance. The epiphany of this peculiarly bleak and pitiless God is the flash-point in all these psalms.

In each poem, we find the same diamond centre: a post-apocalyptic silence, where the nail remains in the hand, and the wound cannot speak. All the light of Pilinszky's religious feeling radiates from the fixity of that crystal. The only possible direction of movement is away from the nailed wound—out of the flesh, and that he rejects.

In this final biological humiliation and solitude, say the poems, nothing can help. Sexual love becomes a howl, or a dumbness groping for somebody—anybody—in the dazzling emptiness. In his love poems, 'he' is separated from 'her' as the flesh is separated from meaning and hope, and as the spirit is separated from any form of consolation. Yet Pilinszky's horror at the physicality and wretchedness of this trap is without any taint of disgust.

And how is it, we might well ask, that this vision of what is, after all, a Universe of Death, an immovable, unalterable horror, where trembling creatures still go uselessly through their motions, how is it that it issues in poems so beautiful and satisfying? How do his few poor objects, his gigantic empty vistas, come to be so unforgettably alive and lit? The convict's scraped skull, the chickens in their wooden cages, the disaster-blanched wall, which recur like features of a prison yard—all have an eerie glowing depth of hieratic beauty, like objects in an early religious painting.

They reveal a place where every cultural support has been torn away, where the ultimate brutality of total war has become natural law, and where man has been reduced to the mere mechanism of his mutilated body. All words seem obsolete or inadequate. Yet out of this apparently final reality rise the poems whose language seems to redeem it, a language in which the symbols of the horror become the sacred symbols of a kind of worship.

These symbols are not redeemed in an unworldly sense. They are redeemed, precariously, in some all-too-human sense, somewhere in the pulsing mammalian nervous system, by a feat of homely consecration: a provisional, last-ditch 'miracle' achieved by means which seem to be never other than 'poetic'.

By this route, Pilinszky's poetry proves itself to be almost a religious activity. But once we have said this we realise it is also a by-product. The main task is something else, deepening a certain kind of attention, refining his submission to his vision of things, which involved Pilinszky's whole life at every moment. And it is true, his personality and his life were as exemplary, for Hungarians, as his poems: they were a single fabric. This insistence of Pilinszky's on paying for his words with his whole way of life attested the authority of his poems. And this is how they come to be an existential challenge to whoever is deeply drawn into them.

It is characteristic that his affinities are not with other poets, but with such figures as Van Gogh, certain of Dostoevsky's characters and above all, perhaps, with Simone Weil. (He translated the *Complete Works* of Simone Weil into Hungarian.) These extreme individuals, the nature of their inner struggles, the temperament verging on the saintly or the suicidal, zigzag like naked lightning through the magnetic atmosphere of Pilinszky's writings. They personify the most vital element, the electrified steely strength under his passivity and gentleness.

If the right hand of his poetic power is his sure grasp of a revealed truth of our final condition, then his left hand, so much more human and hurt, is his mystically intense feeling for the pathos of the sensual world. The intensity is not forceful or strenuous, in any way. It is rather a stillness and at the same time an ecstasy of affliction, a glare of inner exposure, a passivity of transfiguration. At this point, when all the powers of the soul are focused on what is final, and cannot be altered, even though it is horrible, the anguish, it seems, is indistinguishable from joy. The moment closest to extinction turns out to be *the* creative moment.

The result is not comforting. But it is healing. Ghastliness and bliss are weirdly married. The imagery of the central mysteries of Catholicism and the imagery of the camps have become interdependent.

In trying to articulate my impression of the key sensations in Pilinszky's poetry, I realise I have ignored important things, and no doubt missed others completely. 'Poems of such symbolic vitality, like cut jewels, draw their light from every direction.' But after eight or nine years of acquaintance, it seemed worth the attempt to indicate something of the temper and truth of the vision behind these superficially plain and open poems, which our translation has directed itself towards.

Nevertheless, this translation is as close as I could make it. Several Hungarian writers were extremely willing to supply all the word-for-word cribs I needed, and I would like to thank them. It proved most convenient for me, finally, to work with the poet János Csokits, a close friend of long standing, who introduced me to the work of Pilinszky years ago. He has guided me strictly. This translation is really every bit as much his as mine. Very many lines of his rough draft have been impossible to improve, as far as I could judge, and besides that odd inevitability and 'style' which a poet's translation into a language other than his own often seems to have, he retained naturally an unspoiled sense of the flavour and the tone of the originals—that very intriguing quality which is the translator's will-o'-the-wisp, the foreignness and strangeness. That most important thing was something I developed a feeling for, wherever János Csokits captured it, but I could not begin to re-invent it where he did not, or where I had to re-align his wording. The very thing that attracted me to Pilinszky's poems in the first place was their air of simple, helpless accuracy. Nothing conveys that so well as the most literal crib, and I suppose if we had the audacity that is what we should be printing here. As it is, we settled for literalness as a first principle.

One poem in particular which baffled my efforts was 'Apocrypha'. This has all the air of being Pilinszky's summary, ultimate statement. For quite a while I despaired of translating this at all—the eerie splendour of the original is so evident, even in the roughest literal, that any solution seemed tame. János Csokits' word-for-word version, in all its rawness and bracketed shades of meaning, conveyed a vivid sense of this atmosphere and power. In the end I let it rest as printed here, with only the slightest verbal adjustments.

In general, wherever I took a liberty, János Csokits corrected me with infinite pains and lexicographical toil. These translations, then, in the sense of being word for word are close to the originals, and will have served their purpose if they serve as pointers, to help a reader re-imagine the whole thing.

TED HUGHES

1975, 1986

The Desert of Love

FISH IN THE NET

We are tossing in a net of stars.
Fish hauled up to the beach,
gasping in nothingness,
mouths snapping dry void.
Whispering, the lost element
calls us in vain.
Choking among edged stones
and pebbles, we must
live and die in a heap.
Our hearts convulse,
our writhings maim
and suffocate our brother.
Our cries conflict but
not even an echo answers.
We have no reason
to fight and kill
but we must.
So we atone but our atonement
does not suffice.
No suffering
can redeem our hells.
We are tossing in a starry net
and at midnight
maybe we shall lie on the table
of a mighty fisherman.

TRAPEZE AND PARALLEL BARS

Gloomily you turn your back.
In vain my hands weave
the star-studded belt of night
on to your forehead.
Around your throat cluster the gentle
moths of silver fluff.
Intimately you cleave to my body
and laugh. Savagely I hit you.

We run along a radiant ledge.
I trip you, you bound up
snatching at my eyes—
invulnerable beast!
Your face sharpens, and you drop away backwards,
start to plunge wildly, flying
on the trapeze of night
and rising

above the flutter of reality.
A silent ruthless gymnastics.
I cannot even cry out.
With hammering heart, I follow
hurl myself recklessly
and catch your body and fling you down.
Helpless we land in the net
of the quivering stars.

Now I force you to answer:
when did this hunt begin?
Night has clotted in my eyes.
Who started it? Who wanted it? What
will happen to me? What will happen to you?
I love you unconsoled.
We crouch
on the sky's parallel bars—
like convicts condemned.

UNDER THE WINTER SKY

to Tamás Cholnoky

Over my head the stars
jostle their icy flames.
A sky without mercy.
I lean my back to the wall.

Sadness trickles searching
past my orphaned lips.
What happened to my mother's milk?
I smudge my coat.

I am like the stone—
no matter what comes, let it come.
I shall be so obedient and good
I shall fall flat full length.

I shall not deceive myself any longer.
There is nobody to help me.
Suffering cannot redeem me.
No god will protect me.

Nothing could be simpler than this
or more horrible.
The biblical monsters
start slowly towards me.

YOU HAVE HAD TO SUFFER RAIN AND COLD

to György Rónay

So now turn on me, monsters!
Massed, hidden, coming
up through crumbling flues
up, up crying
fire
erupt into this immense
night of mine
which is slowly hardening over you.

Strip me utterly bare
leave me not a thread
rip off my forehead
eyes, lips
for you have had to suffer rain and cold
and you have starved in me, though I too
had to suffer rain and cold and I too
had to starve.

Now let nothing stop you!
Jubilant, faltering shout!
The exultant breakout
of convicts condemned to life—
precarious, blissful moment!
The last! The first!
While I stand
trembling like a
burning forest.

WHAT UNDERGROUND STRUGGLE

I forgot you for days.
It flashed on me one evening
while I lazily
went through my pockets for a cigarette.
Has this starved thicket
of my ravenous nerves devoured you?
Or have I maybe
strangled you with my bare hands.

It makes no difference.
However it happened
the murderer does not think much.
In any case, you are dead.
And you lie, just as if buried in earth,
your grizzled orphaned hair
among my spent cells
in the stiffening slime.

So I believed, mulling stupidly,
till last night. Then a sudden
irresistible force flung me down
beside you. I was unprepared.
A dream had stretched me beside you
and lumped us into one body together
huddling like the poor
on their cramped straw bedding.

And like an acrobat in space
unbalanced by his partner
I went down with you
into the underworld, and though you
had toppled me, I followed
forgetting myself. And shaking
I clutched again what wakefulness
had stolen from me.

As on his last night the condemned man
pulls his cell-mate to him
mourning over him as a second self
of his own fate,
sobbing I held you,
and craving
as we dare to crave only for those
who are both living and dead.

Was it chance that brought us together again?
Or a trap?
Since that moment
I cannot find my place anywhere.
And I keep asking, 'Though you are dead
are you still alive?'
Is your life over or is it hidden
like a smothered fire
in the cellar?

What underground struggle
what blood
is this which reddens my eye corner
from dawn?
The perplexity only grows.
Passion is pitiless.
I thought I had buried you.
Now perhaps you will kill me.

I am afraid. I fear what will happen
if, once again, my dream exhumes you.
I long for you, yet desperately
heap the earth above you.
In my mouth I taste the dirt
of a lurking hell.
Ah God, what hides itself from me?
What is hidden in tomorrow?

SIN

You are still a child but already your limbs
almost wilfully dazzle
in the dawning
system of curves.
And, like a covert smile,
if not your hip, your shoulder
forgets you, and betrays you.
I see you from head to heel.

I look at you, till I can no longer bear it.
One move
and my life starts to slip softly
like a collapsing sand-pit.
You are still fragile—escape
before it reaches you!
Your head topples with a nod.
It was hit by the first blow.

The subsiding years
mine towards you, greedily.
Like starved sticks
the immense forest comes to life.
My nights! The shivering
horde of my nights!
They pounce on you bodily—
a morsel of bread.

They snap your young wrist
they crush your back
they are seeking the ecstasy they never
found with me.
The lost child,
blinding youth!
And they fling you away empty
like a gutted sack.

Is this what you are keeping for me?
I watch you, detached, numb.
Where is the shoulder that flared
the hint of its splendour?
My hands hover, bewildered,
in empty air.
Would you be the one killed?

Would I be the one who killed her?

WORLD GROWN COLD

This world is not my world.
Merely my body's compulsion
as I worm, like a maggot,
deeper and deeper into its bowels.

So I feed on death,
and so death too gets his fill of me.
And my life—for a long time now not mine—
bunches on my heart, like proud scar-flesh.

This is how the refuse crops out
from every creature living,
once he has been chastened, and gladly
casts off useless shame.

And this is how the eternally unknowable
gets its homely look.
As with the leaves in their withering,
my decay embalms me.

It is a world grown cold, a no-man's-land.
And like scrap iron thrown over the top
our hopes
the stars loom dead.

COMPLAINT

Buried alive under the stars
in the mud of nights
do you hear my dumbness?
as if a skyful of birds were approaching.

I keep up this wordless appeal.
Will you ever unearth me
from the perpetual silence
under your foreign skies?

Does my complaint reach you?
Is my siege futile?
All around me glitter
reefs of fear.

Only let me count on you, God.
I want your nearness so much,
shivering
makes the love of loves even fierier.

Bury me in your embrace.
Do not leave me to the frost.
Even if my air is used up
my calling will not tire.

Be the bliss of my trembling
like a tree's leaves:
give a name, give a beautiful name
a pillow to this disintegration.

BY THE TIME YOU COME

I am alone. And by the time you come
I shall be the only one still alive.
Feathers in an empty roost.
Stars intead of a sky.

In my orphanage, unburied,
as on a wintry dump
picking among the rubbish
I keep finding scraps of my life.

And that will be seamless peace.
Even my heart inaudible.
All around me the ecstatic
barriers of silence.

Naked eternity.
And yours, helplessly yours.
A majestic simplicity
created for you, from the first day.

Like a lumpish basketwork dummy
time simply sits, without a word.
Desire has lost its limbs.
It has nothing but a gasping trunk.

By the time you come I shall have lost everything.
No house, no soft bed.
We shall be able to lie undisturbed
in a bare ecstasy.

Only you must not rob me, you must not desert me.
If you are weak, I am finished.
Horrible, then, to awake, in a bed
among pillows, hearing the noise of the street.

HARBACH 1944

to Gábor Thurzó

At all times I see them.
The moon brilliant. A black shaft looms up.
Beneath it, harnessed men
haul a huge cart.

Dragging that giant wagon
which grows bigger as the night grows
their bodies are divided among
the dust, their hunger and their trembling.

They are carrying the road, they are carrying the land,
the bleak potato fields,
and all they know is the weight of everything,
the burden of the skylines

and the falling bodies of their companions
which almost grow into their own
as they lurch, living layers,
treading each other's footsteps.

The villages stay clear of them,
the gateways withdraw.
The distance, that has come to meet them,
reels away back.

Staggering, they wade knee deep
in the low, darkly-muffled clatter
of their wooden clogs
as through invisible leaf litter.

Already their bodies belong to silence.
And they thrust their faces towards the height
as if they strained for a scent
of the far-off celestial troughs

because, prepared for their coming
like an opened stock-yard,
its gates flung savagely back,
death gapes to its hinges.

THE FRENCH PRISONER

If only I could forget that Frenchman.
I saw him, a little before dawn, creeping past our hut
into the dense growth of the back garden
so that he almost merged into the ground.
As I watched he looked back, he peered all round—
at last he had found a safe hideout.
Now his plunder can be all his!
Whatever happens, he'll go no further.

And already he is eating, biting into the turnip
which he must have smuggled out under his rags.
He was gulping raw cattle-turnip!
Yet he had hardly swallowed one mouthful
before it vomited back up.
Then the sweet pulp in his mouth mingled
with joy and revulsion the same
as the happy and unhappy are coupled
in their bodies' ravenous ecstasy.

Only to forget that body, those convulsed shoulder blades,
the hands shrunk to bone,
the bare palm that crammed at his mouth, and clung there
so that it ate, too.
And the shame, desperate, furious,
of the organs savaging each other,
forced to tear from each other
their last shreds of kinship.

The way his clumsy feet had been left out
of the gibbering, bestial elation—
and splayed there, squashed beneath
the torture and rapture of his body.
And his glance—if only I could forget that!
Though he was choking, he kept on
forcing more down his gullet—no matter what—
only to eat—anything—this—that—even himself!

Why go on. Guards came for him.
He had escaped from the nearby prison camp.
And just as I did then, in that garden,
I am strolling here, among garden shadows, at home.
I look into my notes and quote:
'If only I could forget that Frenchman. . . .'
And from my ears, from my eyes, my mouth
the scorching memory roars at me:

'I am hungry!' And suddenly I feel
the everlasting hunger
that poor creature has long since forgotten
and which no earthly nourishment can lessen.
He lives on me. And more and more hungrily!
And I am less and less sufficient for him.
And now he, who would have eaten anything,
is yelling for my heart.

ON THE WALL OF A KZ-LAGER

Where you have fallen, you stay.
In the whole universe, this is your place.
Just this single spot.
But you have made this yours utterly.

The countryside evades you.
House, mill, poplar,
each thing strives to be free of you
as if it were mutating in nothingness.

But now it is you who stay.
Did we blind you? You continue to watch us.
Did we rob you? You enriched yourself.
Speechless, speechless, you testify against us.

PASSION OF RAVENSBRÜCK

He steps out from the others.
He stands in the square silence.
The prison garb, the convict's skull
blink like a projection.

He is horribly alone.
His pores are visible.
Everything about him is so gigantic,
everything is so tiny.

And this is all.
               The rest—
the rest was simply
that he forgot to cry out
before he collapsed.

FRANKFURT

In the river bank, an empty sandpit—
all that summer we took the refuse there.
Gliding between villas and gardens
we came to a bridge. Then a dip of the road
and the wooden fence of the racetrack.
A few jolts, and the truck began to slow down.
But even before the brakes could tighten
the first surge of hunger overwhelmed us.

Among the spilling buckets and the bursting sacks—
horror of the spines, bent into position!
Then among those toppled crates began
the pitiless pre-censorship,
interrogating the gristles of the offal.
And there, on all fours, hunger
could not stomach its own fury,
but revolted and surrendered.

They were lost in the dust and filth.
The whole truck shook, howling.
The swill clogged their hearts.
It swamped their consciousness.
They burrowed into the depths of the filled bins
till mouths and eyes were caked.
They drowned in that living sludge
and there, upside down, they were resurrected.

And brought back, scrap by scrap,
what had been utterly lost with them,
wringing their salvation, drunkenly,
out of the gouged mush—
but before their joy could be consummated
the poison of understanding stirred.
First, only the bitterness in their mouths,
then their hearts tasted the full misery.

Abruptly, they backed from the crush. Almost sober
they watched how this drunkenness—
betraying their despair—
possessed their whole being.
But then again, reckless, they abandoned themselves,
now merely enduring, till their organs,
sating themselves, should have completed
the last mistakes of pleasure.

Only to get away—no matter where!
Only to get out, now!
The glowing pack drove us from them
without a flash! They did not even touch us.
All around—the blank walls of the pit.
Only to get home! Probably a steamer
went past quite close by on the river below
and its smoke and soot screened perfectly

the steep, crooked exit. Out across the field!
Bounding eagerly over the mounds
on to the flaming concrete. Then the villas!
The green world streaming back!
The wooden fence of the racecourse.
And after the volley of gaps between the palings
the hot scent, swooning from the gardens!
Then all at once—the shock of loneliness!

In a moment the splendour of the foliage burned out—
its flame hung darkly to the road.
And our faces, and our hands, darkened.
And with us, the paradise.
While behind us, between the jouncing cans
and the tattered dusty trees
emerged the crepuscular city
of Frankfurt—1945.

IMPROMPTU

For months now, I have been wandering
aimlessly. Endlessly.
A sweet deadly sunstroke
tortures and blinds me, night and day.

Where do these visitations come from?
Somebody steps from the water
dazzling, young,
slips through the abrupt darkness.

Her smile lifts toward the shore.
Far off, a few sails blaze.
The vertical noon heat
showers down on the litter of bathing huts.

Details and trivia.
A single flower in the soft wind
turning over and over, as in the fingers
of a mute and wondering baby.

And the melodies. Through all those rooms
the same wash of melodies,
as though the barefoot sea were roaming
among their walls.

But most beautiful of all—the lovers!
Their manes glowing out of the shadows
the last beautiful tent of their modesty.

The lovers. And the twilight.
The rows of houses, sinking into the dark.
And over the houses, on the sand,
a tower's ponderous mass.

Who could have dreamed up anything so sad.

THE DESERT OF LOVE

A bridge, and a hot concrete road—
the day is emptying its pockets,
laying out, one by one, all its possessions.
You are quite alone in the catatonic twilight.

A landscape like the bed of a wrinkled pit,
with glowing scars, a darkness which dazzles.
Dusk thickens. I stand numb with brightness
blinded by the sun. This summer will not leave me.

Summer. And the flashing heat.
The chickens stand, like burning cherubs,
in the boarded-up, splintered cages.
I know their wings do not even tremble.

Do you still remember? First there was the wind.
And then the earth. Then the cage.
Flames, dung. And now and again
a few wing-flutters, a few empty reflexes.

And thirst. I asked for water.
Even today I hear that feverish gulping,
and helplessly, like a stone, bear
and quench the mirages.

Years are passing. And years. And hope
is like a tin-cup toppled into the straw.

REVELATIONS VIII.7

and God sees the burning heaven
and against it birds flying
and he sees sinking deeper and deeper
those too weak to cross the disc of fire

and from end to end
in a redness of copper broken to fragments
where a man hoeing will never be found again
he sees the earth and once again the earth

the desert and the chaos
and a horse and cart searching to wade out
but God sees there is no way
or road or hope to break from this vision!

APOCRYPHA

1

Everything will be forsaken then

The silence of the heavens will be set apart
and forever apart
the broken-down fields of the finished world,
and apart
the silence of dog-kennels.
In the air a fleeing host of birds.
And we shall see the rising sun
dumb as a demented eye-pupil
and calm as a watching beast.

But keeping vigil in banishment
because that night
I cannot sleep I toss
as the tree with its thousand leaves
and at dead of night I speak as the tree:

Do you know the drifting of the years
the years over the crumpled fields?
Do you understand the wrinkle
of transience? Do you comprehend
my care-gnarled hands? Do you know
the name of orphanage? Do you know
what pain treads the unlifting darkness
with cleft hooves, with webbed feet?
The night, the cold, the pit. Do you know
the convict's head twisted askew?
Do you know the caked troughs, the tortures
of the abyss?

The sun rose. Sticks of trees blackening
in the infra-red of the wrathful sky.

So I depart. Facing devastation
a man is walking, without a word.
He has nothing. He has his shadow.
And his stick. And his prison garb.

2

And this is why I learned to walk! For these
belated bitter steps.

Evening will come, and night will petrify
above me with its mud. Beneath closed eyelids
I do not cease to guard this procession
these fevered shrubs, their tiny twigs.
Leaf by leaf, the glowing little wood.
Once Paradise stood here.
In half-sleep, the renewal of pain:
to hear its gigantic trees.

Home—I wanted finally to get home—
to arrive as he in the Bible arrived.
My ghastly shadow in the courtyard.
Crushed silence, aged parents in the house.
And already they are coming, they are calling me,
my poor ones, and already crying,
and embracing me, stumbling—
the ancient order opens to readmit me.
I lean out on the windy stars.

If only for this once I could speak with you
whom I loved so much. Year after year
yet I never tired of saying over
what a small child sobs
into the gap between the palings,
the almost choking hope
that I come back and find you.
Your nearness throbs in my throat.
I am agitated as a wild beast.

I do not speak your words,
the human speech. There are birds alive
who flee now heart-broken
under the sky, under the fiery sky.
Forlorn poles stuck in a glowing field,
and immovably burning cages.
I do not understand the human speech,
and I do not speak your language.
My voice is more homeless than the word!
I have no words.

            Its horrible burden
tumbles down through the air—
a tower's body emits sounds.

You are nowhere. How empty the world is.
A garden chair, and a deckchair left outside.
Among sharp stones my clangorous shadow.
I am tired. I jut out from the earth.

3

God sees that I stand in the sun.
He sees my shadow on stone and on fence.
He sees my shadow standing
without a breath in the airless press.

By then I am already like the stone;
a dead fold, a drawing of a thousand grooves,
a good handful of rubble
is by then the creature's face.

And instead of tears, the wrinkles on the faces
trickling, the empty ditch trickles down.

QUATRAIN

Nails asleep under frozen sand.
Nights soaked in poster-loneliness.
You left the light on in the corridor.
Today my blood is shed.

UNDER A PORTRAIT

The sun chills in the graphite of dusk.
With its deeps and its expanses
the soundless sea gleams into my face.
I am old. I believe in nothing.

I am old. On my broken-up face
only the frightening emptiness of the water.
The granite dust of nightfall. Only
the brutal veil, the lace-work of pores.

The surf. And now the soft night's
unhappy noises. Blind insect
in the darkening cardboard box,
I am alone, orphaned of everything.

And alone in the bottomless bed.
Alone among pillows.
Alone in my unending loneliness.
Like the sea itself. Like the earth.

COLD WIND

unpeopled rock, my spine lying
without memories, without me
in the extinct ashes of millions of years.

Cold wind still blowing.

UNFINISHED PAST

to Ted Hughes

It arrives, it stiffens
on the ashen silent wall:
the moon. A single immense blow.
Its core is a death-stillness.

It shatters the roads
the moonlight shatters them.
It rips the wall apart.
White gushes over the black.

The black day splits with lightning.
And lightning. And lightning.
Cataracts of white and black.
You comb your hair in the magnetic tempest.

You comb your hair in the flashing silence.
In a mirror more vigilant than the unfinished past.

You comb your hair in the mirror
silently, as in a coffin of glass.

NOVEMBER ELYSIUM

Convalescence. You hang back, at the verge
of the garden. Your background
a peaceful yellow wall's monastery silence.
A tame little wind starts out across the grass. And now,
as if hands assuaged them with holy oils,
your five open wounds, your five senses
feel their healing and are eased.

You are timid. And exultant. Yes,
with your childishly translucent limbs,
in the shawl and coat grown tall,
you are like Alyosha Karamazov.

And like those gentle ones, over yonder,
who are like the child, yes, you are like them.
And as happy too, because
you do not want anything any more.
Only to gleam like the November sun,
and exhale fragrance, lightly as a fir-cone.
Only to bask, like the blest.

Szigliget, November 1958

EPILOGUE

to Pierre Emmanuel

Remember? On the faces.
Remember? The empty ditch.
Remember? It's streaming down.
Remember? I stand in the sun.

You read the Paris Journal.
Since then, winter has come. Winter's night.
You lay the table beside me.
You make the bed in the moonlight.

Catching your breath, you undress
in the dark of the bare house.
You let down your skirt, and take off your blouse.
Your back is a bare tombstone.

Image of wretched strength.
Is anybody here?
                     A waking dream:
unanswered, I cross
the rooms lying in the depths of mirrors.

Is this my face? This face?
The light, the silence, and the judgement are shattered
as this stone, my face, hurtles towards me
out of the snow-white mirror!

And the horsemen! The horsemen!
Darkness oppresses me. The lamplight hurts me.
A slack thread of water plays
on the motionless china.

I rattle at the closed doors.
Your room is dark as a shaft.
The walls glare with cold.
I smudge my weeping on the wall.

You snow-heaped house-tops, help me!
Now it is night. Now let every orphaned thing
shine out, before there arises
the sun of nothingness. And you, in vain,

shine! I lean my head to the wall.
From all around me the dead city
holds towards me, mercy towards the dead,
a handful of snow.

I loved you! A shout. A sigh.
A cloud in flight.
And through the slush, under breaking dawn,
at a heavy torrential trot, come the horsemen.

INTROITUS

Who, now, shall open the closed book?
Who shall make the first cut in unbroken
time? Turning from dawn to dawn,
lifting the pages and letting them fall.

Which of us shall dare reach into
the flames of the hidden? Who shall dare grope
among the dense leaves of the sealed book?
And how shall he dare, with his bare hand?

Which of us is without fear? Who would not fear
when even God's eyes shut
and all the angels fall flat
and every creature darkens?

Among us, only the Lamb has no fear.
He alone, the Lamb who was killed.
And he is jogging along on the sea of glass.
He climbs up on to the throne. He opens the book.

FABLE

Detail from *KZ-Oratorio: Dark Heaven*

Once upon a time
there was a lonely wolf
lonelier than the angels.

He happened to come to a village.
He fell in love with the first house he saw.

Already he loved its walls
the caresses of its bricklayers.
But the window stopped him.

In the room sat people.
Apart from God nobody ever
found them so beautiful
as this child-like beast.

So at night he went into the house.
He stopped in the middle of the room
and never moved from there any more.

He stood all through the night, with wide eyes
and on into the morning when he was beaten to death.

BIG CITY ICONS

Noon, 12
Uninhabitable! they shout, Uninhabitable!

3 a.m. dawn
We start out towards a pile of stones.
A bird flies up from behind it.

Museum
In the centre
of a diamond-empty museum
a brooch blazes.
It ravages. It perpetuates.
Where do we get to, from this blaze?

The motionless galleries?
Your empty cuffs, maybe?
The June afternoon
ravages. It perpetuates.

Avenues of September!
My love! My love! My love!
The avenues come to a stop.
Universal wounds in the garden.

You have attempted
what nobody dared, you poor orphan!
May the night's
eternally-empty monstrance
brighten for you.

Choir
The Creature pleads
sinks down, surrenders.
The Creature—the One That
Pleads—opens itself.

VAN GOGH

1

They undressed in the dark.
They lay down, they fell asleep.
While you, in the glare,
wept and pondered.

2

Night was falling.
In the ramshackle heat
the sun came paper close.
Everything stopped.
A ball of iron also stood there.

3

'Lamb of the world, lupus in fabula,
I am burning
in the glass cabinet of the present tense.'

THE PASSION

Only the warmth of the slaughter-house,
its geranium pungency, its soft shellac,
only the sun exists.

In a glass-cased silence
the butcher-boys wash down. Yet what has happened
somehow cannot even now finish.

JUST LIKE THE EARTH

Just like the earth where I shall soar
unmoving, and crumble;
just like the water, so near
is the solemn hour of weeping.

AS I WAS

As I was at the start
so, all along, I have remained.
The way I began, so I will go on to the end.
Like the convict who, returning
to his village, goes on being silent.
Speechless he sits in front of his glass of wine.

CRIME AND PUNISHMENT

to Sheryl Sutton

The walled-in imagination
continues to repeat it—

The face is still there
throned in the electric chair of the moment
the nape dipped in cliff
the beautiful hand—
the porous skin of your presence.

And still the summer goes on.

Let down your sceptre, Queen.

EXHORTATION

Not the respiration. The gasping.
Not the wedding table. The falling
scraps, the chill, the shadows.
Not the gesture. Not the hysteria.
The silence of the hook is what you must note.

Record
what your city, the everlasting city
has watched,
with its towers, its roofs,
its living and dead citizens,
to this very hour.

Then you may make known,
perhaps, even in your day,
what is alone
worthy the annunciation,

Scribe

then perhaps you will not have passed in vain.

THE PRAYER OF VAN GOGH

The battle lost in the field.
The air held by invaders.
Birds, the sun, and again birds.
By night what will be left of me?

At night only the row of lamps
the yellow wall of dry mud
and from the bottom of the garden, through trees,
like a row of candles, the windows,

where I too dwelt and do not dwell,
the house where I lived and do not live,
the roof which tucked me in safely.
Ah God, then you covered me up safely.

MY COAT OF ARMS

Grace and joy have ripened
together with what is generally called
misery.

Oil and nails could be my coat of arms.
But what motto should I set to it?

Maybe that I understand everything—
the drifting of the clouds, the heads of pigs
flattened against the plank hard as a press.

But even this, what does it amount to?
We ourselves, in the end,
are forced into the press. To complete
the sentence.

GRADUALLY

As the nothingness soothes over
the ditches of the death-struggle,
as the fields after a blizzard
calm down and find their way home again,
somehow, in just such a gradual way,
growing plain and simple, unfolds
the dialogue of God and man,
destruction and birth.

ENOUGH

Creation, no matter how vast,
is more cramped than a roost.
From here to there. Stone, tree, house.
I potter about, come early, come too late.

Yet, now and again, some person enters
and in a moment everything has opened—
the sight of a face, a presence is enough,
and the wallpaper starts to bleed.

Enough, yes, enough a hand
as it stirs a cup of coffee
or as it 'withdraws from the introduction'
and enough
that we forget the place
the airless row of windows, yes,
that returning, at night, to our room
we accept the unacceptable.

STRAIGHT LABYRINTH

How will it be, that flying back
of which only symbols tell—
altar, shrine, handshake,
homecoming, embrace,
table laid in the grass, under the trees,
where there is no first and no last guest—
how will it be, in the end how will it be
the wide-winged ascending plunge
back into the flaming
common nest of the focus?—I don't know,
and yet, if I know anything,
I know this—this hot corridor,
this labyrinth straight as an arrow
and fuller and fuller, freer and freer
the fact that we are flying.

MEDITATION

Is the art of pariahs possible? Can the animal unassumingness, which is stuck in man, hope for words, for a shape? A rhythm which, like the dogs in summer, merely pulsates, is it possible? Spirit, poor beyond comparison, bleak as stone, not in our consciousness but pinned to the earth? Language, that had not the force to put out its sprays, its foliage?

Because there is here thirst of a kind, which nobody ever gave a drink. Misery, its trunk heaving more and more horribly.

His shall be all the power and the glory.

STAVROGIN TAKES HIS LEAVE

'I am bored. Give me my cloak, please.
Before you commit anything
think of the rose-garden,
or, rather, of a single rose-tree,
of one single rose, gentlemen.'

JEWEL

The antelope is looking at herself
in a perfectly-fashioned mirror.
Hanging at her neck: a gem.

Of her we say: beautiful as a tapestry.
We say: you just go on looking at yourself
and we shall bear children, be born, die.

We whisper things of this kind
to the antelope living in madness.

STAVROGIN RETURNS

'You have not remembered the rose-garden.
You have done what you should not have done.

From now on you shall be hunted,
and lonely as a butterfly-collector.
All of you will end up under glass.

Under the glass pane, pinned on needle points
glitter, glitter the host of butterflies.
It is you who glitter, gentlemen.

I am afraid. Give me my cloak, please.'

PATHOGRAPHY AND SWANSONG

A white arm from a snow-white mirror,
thin beautiful arm, with persistent force,
with a cold sponge, from the cold glass
tries since eternity to make somebody,
somebody or something vanish.

TWO

Two white weights are watching each other,
two snow-white and pitch-black weights.
I am because I am not.

AQUARIUM

My sister in the aquarium
draws back in among the algae.
Day and night we are searching where she is.
Aunts, children, grandchild.
We look for her in the slimy, unfamiliar,
foliage-leaf grave-cemetery.

She is crouching on the bed. Debris.
Trembles. Wakes up. Starts up.
Lights a cigarette. Speaks. Addresses us. Nobody.
Like a fish-bird
flutters and wrings her fins,
trembles and pulsates. Her fish-bird's eye
does not search our eyes, only
drills holes. It does not matter where to,
only that it should be a hole, in anybody, in anything,
against us, against me, against herself,
at any price, a hole.

CRATER

We have met. We keep meeting.
In the tobacconist's. At an auction.
You were rummaging for something. You shift
something. I would like to flee. I stay.
I light a cigarette. You leave.

You step down. You climb up.
I climb up. I step down.
Cigarette. You pace; I pace.
We march on the spot; like a murderer
I wade in your walking.

It is bird-twittering as
you blame me for my birth.
That we stand here. Then in a dead backwater
of a street-section my muttering
begins to roll tumbling down from your gigantic
limbs and from that triumphant
and blinding something
which is already not you.

Your rejection has affected me,
this adultery slash inscribed in stone,
so that ever since
my look—two pebbles—
rolls and rolls
in a snow-white crater. My eyes,
two eyes, bounce: my salvation.

HOMMAGE À SHERYL SUTTON I

In the narrowest possible space
you achieved the forbidden.
You marvelled at the ceremony
which is a slaughter-house, though it has no dimension,
reaches to the elbow, though it is not in time.

Only later did you hear what
you have withheld, then entering the garden
you were astonished by the magic of the full moon.

JÁNOS PILINSZKY: A VERY DIFFERENT POET

Pilinszky is different. Everybody is different but some are even more so. Pilinszky is more different in that way in Hungarian poetry and within poetry as such; that is, he is different in fact, he is genuinely different, deeply deviant, rare and improbable, a white antelope, an element beyond the periodic table. When he walked down the street, one of those dark Budapest streets of the fifties, in his short coat, too tight around the shoulders, he walked like a persecuted legend. That is just what he was. A persecuted legend, pushed out of literature and completely unknown; perhaps fellow-dwellers in the catacombs whispered his name, passing it from mouth to mouth and ear to ear.

How did that situation in his life, which is as important to his verse as the war was to his experience, come about? A few facts from his biography are needed to answer this.

János Pilinszky was born in Budapest in 1921. He always lived in Budapest, in the left-bank Inner City. No, not in the fashionable metropolitan centre, but in the modest, middle-class ancient kernel of the town. That is where he lived, on the second floor of an old tenement with uncovered corridors, with his widowed mother, his sister and her family and a few other elderly female relatives. 'I only like troglodytic homes', he once said. That is what his home was like, a true cave, with narrow windows facing the street and heavy, dark curtains and furniture. The chimes of the church of the Mary Ward Sisters were the sound most likely to filter in from the outside world. His Catholicism was part of his family heritage; and as long as he could he stuck close to his family's protective cave walls. His mother's death meant a serious change in his life, a split in the family protective caul, adulthood that could no longer be delayed. The outside world was not for him.

Some of his verses had been published early, even in the best literary journals, such as *Magyar Csillag* (edited by Gyula Illyés), the wartime successor of *Nyugat*, and this lent them a certain standing. These precious poems that outlined the Pilinszky-to-be attracted notice. Some looked on him as a promising talent even then. But there was a war on and the poet received one of the last call-up papers in 1944, by which time his feeble physique no longer meant exemption. He went west with his company, to wartime Germany. This was the experience that determined his work. Back home again he took part in the bubbling, exciting three years of Hungarian literature that lasted from 1945 to 1948. He moved mainly in the *Újhold* circle, being the poetry editor of the journal of the younger writers of that name. The period of what is euphemistically called the personality cult followed, a time to keep quiet. Pilinszky, like a good many other Hungarian writers, could not publish for around ten years. His position—financial and intellectual—balanced on the frontier between being and non-being. The large family found it difficult to support itself. The poet tried to make a living doing odd jobs for the Catholic press, and translations and proof-reading, he was given out of pity. He corrected the proofs of the books of those poets who appeared at that time.

This period came to an end in 1956, with another explosion. There was gunfire in the streets of Budapest once again. Later the thaw started. Circumstances changed and the silenced writers, Pilinszky amongst them, were being published once more.

His most important volumes of verse are: *Trapéz és korlát* (Trapeze and Parallel Bars) which appeared in 1946 and earned him the Baumgarten Prize. *Harmadnapon* (On the Third Day) was published in 1959, the first volume after the years of silence. Then: *Nagyvárosi ikonok* (Big City Icons), 1970, *Szálkák* (Splinters), 1972, *Végkifejlet* (Denouement), 1974 and *Kráter* (Crater), 1976. He also published prose or works that can be called prose, reflections, articles, conversations with a black actress, a member of Robert Wilson's Paris company: *Beszélgetések Sheryl Suttonnal* (Conversations with Sheryl Sutton), poetic works for the stage and oratorios. Lately he experimented with writing a novel. Two volumes of his verses appeared in English, *Selected Poems* (Carcanet New Press, 1976) translated by Ted Hughes and János Csokits, and *Crater* (Anvil Press Poetry, 1978) translated by Peter Jay. Many poems by him, indeed whole volumes, appeared in numerous languages, such as French, German, Norwegian and Finnish.

From the mid-sixties Pilinszky underwent considerable change. His style was transformed though his message stayed the same. He had been one who wrote little and became someone who wrote more, but it was chiefly his way of life and his personality that changed. As his popularity grew at home and abroad his circle of friends suddenly grew much larger, an inward-looking man seemingly became an outward-looking one, and the hermit turned into a globe-trotter. He spent a lot of time in Paris, at Pierre Emmanuel's invitation, but he travelled the length and breadth of Europe and America as well. It was not travel as such that interested him, or people: what drove him was some sort of feverish or nervous desire to communicate. It was not his basic relationship to the world that changed but his rôle on the stage of life.

What this transformation, this new rôle really meant, what its causes were, and what its effects, is still too difficult to judge. One thing is certain, however, the identity maintained through change which signifies that great poet and that extraordinary phenomenon János Pilinszky.

Everyone has a right to his own youthful portrait, to that moment in life where youth and maturity meet, where he most acutely identifies with his self; he has a right to the high noon of his identity. Now that the poet is allegedly dead—though I do not believe it—that is the moment I aim at, that is the point which I am trying to train sights at. That. There. Up there, or rather down, or up and down, on the badly paved sidewalk of Molnár Street or the bumpy mattress of my Kékgolyó Street flat, where he walked, sat, lived, on inner-city corridors, or with a small black coffee in front of him in an always badly lit espresso. His white hand and white face lit up the tunnels of the fifties like a Davy lamp.

High noon then was down below, that chosen moment of the portrait which I am trying to sketch with staggering lines, all the time running off the paper into my own life, and his life, forcing myself back onto this ridiculous piece of paper which I am writing on. High noon was down below, somewhere deep down, in a tunnel, mine or sewer, where the outer nadir and the inner zenith coincided, that is if one may discriminate between 'outer' and 'inner' precisely in his case. Let's take the outer nadir first. This low point in his circumstances was already the second in Pilinszky's life. The first was the war, soldiering, serving as an anti-aircraft gunner, staying in Germany, wandering amid the mire of death-camps, Hungarian soldiers jumping out into the road, prostrating themselves to jeeps, begging to be made prisoner, but they were not because there was no room, a bite of bread had to be put off, the movement of 'the hands shrunk to bone, / the bare palm that crammed at his mouth, and clung there / so that it ate, too.' The second low point was the fifties: *Trapéz és korlát* appeared in the brief pause between the two.

In that first volume he is already complete—the finish is on him—in a certain sense. 'Harbach 1944' and a few more future basic poems of the new Hungarian literature are already there. And, first of all, what is there—naturally in his great volume *Harmadnapon*—is the meeting of the poet and his subject, the one most usually used to describe Pilinszky, anti-fascism, the incomparable poetic heat of the experience of the death-camp. After all this was our experience, that of all of us, of our generation and of the whole world: to write verse after Auschwitz, to survey and stammer about the war and its deepest burden and symbol, the suprahuman wounds of the concentration camps. We did our bit all right. Usually the way one ought to, balancing on the edge of propositions, throwing in a stone-lot of silence, brushing it with the corner of the eye of our poetic glance, all that could only be made visible in that way. One could list masterpieces of poems of this sort from all over the world.

But Pilinszky's way was different. He undertook something impossible, something poetically dangerous. He plunged straight into it, *in medias res*, and described what it was like. *He steps out from the others. / He stands in the square silence.* ('Passion of Ravensbrück') *Staggering, they wade knee deep / in the low, darkly-muffled clatter / of their wooden clogs / as through invisible leaf litter.* ('Harbach 1944') *Like a lumpish basketwork dummy / time simply sits, without a word.* ('By the Time You Come') *And there, on all fours, hunger / could not stomach its own fury, / but revolted and surrendered.* ('Frankfurt') ... *on the ashen silent wall.* ('Unfinished Past') *Nails asleep under frozen sand.* ('Quatrain')

I do not mean the quotations to be quotations, only reminders, mumbled half-lines. What is needed to produce such description, to make it what it is, can only be made clear at great length. What is needed in the first place is the savage strength of his own slim windswept body. For he was strong of course, narrowly aggressive, like a laser beam. What was needed for his texts was the highly condensed load of his truck-sentences, the concrete sleepers of his poetic rail-system, and chiefly the ability to choose, the ongoing, ascetic renunciation of words, the cramped luxury of the hunt for the 'single word' that lasted months and years, or decades. 'He wrote little', that is he wrote a great deal, stuffing the dimension of 'much' into what was little.

All that—and much else—was needed for him to write the supreme poetry of the death-camp experience. But that was not enough. Why was it just Pilinszky who was best able to tell the story of the scandal of the century, he who was not even present in it? No, participation is not the key word, but identity, the preparedness from the start of his person for this very experience. This is where he is special, that is the nature of his otherness, beyond the periodic table; he recognised the death-camp as his imaginings come true, the way a space-creature recognises the cold of space. In the same way that the physical and mental realm of the proletariat was, up to a certain degree, the 'form' of Attila József, so the camps were Pilinszky's form. They were his furnished world of self. He had so little to do with the everyday world, he was as much a stranger on the anthropomorphic earth as a man could be, or perhaps could not be, and it was precisely here, and through this, that his being reached and swam into the non-anthropomorphic final judgement of the camps, that which is beyond the comprehensible. The people of Florence looked on Dante as we did on Pilinszky, as a man who had been through hell. But he had not only been through, he lived right in it; in a darkness swept through from time to time by rays of keen grace. It was there inside him before he experienced it and after he experienced it, he carried inside him its cistern-prison, in Váci Street, in Paris and in London hotels. He had a single message, single and huge: suffering. But since suffering too is of many kinds, has many tricks and torture chambers, his was the expelled, the waif, the extreme, the end-of-the-world, the borderline, in fact unnameable suffering or hell; neither common nor private names exhaust it. No, let us not hurry with captions to label the creature's torments. It is perhaps only religion that offers examples—and words—for this sort of absence of place. His Catholicism was that huge, all-embracing analogy-system into which he was able to fit.

It was this existential suffering, this figure descended to hell that met the wars and gas chambers of the twentieth century. And through this, through the wild metabolic decay of the meeting, the extreme, the other, the no-place figure turned into a paradigm and Pilinszky's poetry into a burning public question. It became apparent that the world resembled Pilinszky, his dimension, his prisons and his apocalypse. That which is only the sky, and only a dark heaven, seemed to have been able to receive it, all of a sudden became general, like a blade of grass, like a goods truck, like a wound. The poet and his century—its darkest centre—were joined together, his validity became historical and then grew beyond that.

What he did was to write his poem 'Apocrypha'. 'Apocrypha' speaks volumes, we all know that, and so did he. 'Apocrypha' carries unexpected, new movements into the trembling but basically unmoving, static nature of his poetry, condensing what went before and what followed. Associations, the distance between adjective and subject, the tectonic faults of the structure, the new-fangled level of 'where I am speaking from' convey the suggestion of a personal avant-garde, while the poem doesn't budge from the poetic rock of authenticity even an inch. The screeching calm of the last judgement flows from this last judgement-poem, and all our century does is to lend it the stage sets. The temporal and the eternal, the eschatological and personal, the human and suprahuman all tumble into each other in it. Pilinszky the poet of the beyond, the meta-poet, gives us the beyond, a despair placed high, as it were switching the ancient spatial experience of man, in which the bright is high up and the dark down below. Just as at that time, at the bottom of the fifties, he made the zenith and the nadir coincide, with the thin, white gestures of the Pilinszky hand covering suffering with the sacredness of suffering, which is the antechamber of grace.

Pilinszky added a dimension to our lives (all our lives, now, the life of poetry), he enriched us with want, with being lost, the dearth of existence pared down to the bone. The extraordinary catharsis of his poetic power arched over such dearth. It would be good to look now into those places to which he opened a breach, look in through the inner doors of the ante chamber, to those places where destruction is spread out like the sky.

ÁGNES NEMES NAGY

translated by Rudolf Fischer

Poetry in translation from Anvil

Charles Baudelaire
THE POEMS IN PROSE
translated by Francis Scarfe

Bei Dao
THE AUGUST SLEEPWALKER
translated by Bonnie S. McDougall

Elisabeth Borchers
FISH MAGIC
translated by Anneliese Wagner

Paul Celan
POEMS OF PAUL CELAN
translated by Michael Hamburger

Arthur Rimbaud
A SEASON IN HELL *and other poems*
translated by Norman Cameron
with a preface by Michael Hamburger

Yannis Ritsos
EXILE AND RETURN
translated by Edmund Keeley

Vittorio Sereni
SELECTED POEMS OF VITTORIO SERENI
translated by Marcus Perryman and Peter Robinson

Daniel Weissbort (ed.)
THE POETRY OF SURVIVAL

Sándor Weöres
ETERNAL MOMENT
edited by Miklós Vajda
translated by Edwin Morgan, William Jay Smith and others

A catalogue of our publications is available on request

The Desert of Love